T0279243

THE INVENTORS

THE FRENCH LIST

René Char

THE INVENTORS

AND OTHER POEMS

Translated by Mark Hutchinson

LONDON NEW YORK CALCUTTA

**PAP
TAGORE**

www.bibliofrance.in

The work is published with the support of the
Publication Assistance Programmes of the Institut français

Seagull Books, 2015

Original poems © Editions Gallimard, Paris, 1950, 1962, 1962, 1971,
1975, 1977, 1979, 1983, 1985, 1988

English translation © Mark Hutchinson, 2015

ISBN   978 0 8574 2 324 5

British Library Cataloguing-in-Publication Data
A catalogue record for this book
is available from the British Library

Typeset by Seagull Books, Calcutta, India
Printed and bound by Maple Press, York, Pennsylvania, USA

CONTENTS

ACKNOWLEDGEMENTS

Grateful acknowledgement is made to the editors of the following publications, in which some of the translations, often in slightly different form, first appeared: *Pequod*, *Selected Poems of René Char* (New Directions, 1992), *The Times Literary Supplement*, *Twentieth-Century French Poems* (Faber, 2002). Several of the poems were privately printed as chapbooks: 'The Inventors' in 1988; 'The Schoolgirl's Companion' in 1990; and 'Fontis', 'Society' and 'Newsletter' as *Three Poems* in 1994. The *Lascaux* poems were first published by Peter Baldwin's Delos Press in 1998.

Of the influential post-war French poets, René Char must be the one least familiar to English-speaking readers today. If he figures at all on their map of twentieth-century poetry, it tends to be as the author of just one book—his Resistance journal, *Feuillets d'Hypnos*—and, often as not, at second-hand: as the 'philosopher–poet' admired by Heidegger and Hannah Arendt, or a footnote to the work of Paul Celan, the first of his German translators and the recipient of one of the most arresting author-to-author inscriptions in literature. It's not that translations haven't been made before: they have, on half a dozen occasions, and in some bulk. But with a few exceptions (Richard Wilbur, W. S. Merwin, Patricia Terry, James Wright) and one lovely but little-known version by Seamus Heaney, they have been of the *mot-à-mot* variety—cribs, English texts which hunker down in the shadow of the facing page and, while more or less faithful to the letter of the French, neglect nearly everything else that makes a poem a poem— timbre, cadence, syntax, pace.

We needn't be too sentimental about this. A lot of Char's work is written in a high style at odds with the anti-Romantic emphasis of most modern poetry, and while the best of his writing is admirably vivid and concise (Northrop Frye once suggested it be 'swallowed at a gulp' like a Bloody Mary 'and allowed to explode inside'), many of his poems are embroiled in a language so gnarled and baroque, so bristling with metaphor, as to be all but impenetrable; even if I wanted to, I wouldn't know how to go about translating them. Then, suddenly, you turn a page and everything is out in the open, each word exactly in its place. It might be a small lyric like 'Fontis', for example, about the melancholy foundations of creation, or a more elaborate and intricately textured poem like 'The Epte Woods' (whose maze of imagery, aptly enough, evokes a love entanglement); or a luminous and tender prose poem (which D. H. Lawrence would have admired) about the outcast from the garden, the viper; or, arguably the finest of all Char's poems, 'The Inventors', a poem as immediately memorable to me when I first read it twenty-five years ago as some of the better-known poems with which it invites comparison— Eliot's 'Journey of the Magi', say, or Cavafy's 'Waiting for the Barbarians'.

These are the poems presented here. It's a smallish gathering, forty poems in all, but one that, together with the *Hypnos* book and some of his occasional prose, could be said to form the heart of Char's work—or that part of it, at least, that is patient of English translation. Some of the poems I have chosen are well known; others, particularly those from his later collections, less so. All were translated first and foremost for the joy of it, but in part also to try and clarify in my own mind the concerns of this difficult but, for all his obvious shortcomings, important poet. If Char's work were likened to a forest, the poems I have chosen would be the clearings.

Char spent his early years writing violently anti-authoritarian poems under the banner of Surrealism, and though he always rejected the idea that poetry should serve a cause, many of his poems have a marked political undertow. Political in the sense, that is, not of Brecht (whom he admired) or Louis Aragon (whom he came to despise because of his subservience to Moscow), but of Shelley or Blake, both of whom appear in a small but striking book of translations, centred around the figure of Mandelstam, that he put together with Tina Jolas towards the end of his life. Political in the sense of bound up with the common weal and the common woe, and with poetry as an instrument of resistance and redress.

There are two or three big themes related to this. The first of these, the fulcrum about which all Char's work turns, is the Heracletian notion of strife or conflict as the foundation of the world, a balancing of equal and opposite forces without which everything from good governance to attraction between the sexes would cease to exist. When that balance is disrupted, the poetic imagination will step in to redress it—an act illustrated in particularly dramatic form by the metaphysical husbandry explored in his Resistance journal, but also celebrated in several of the poems here: in the gainsaying of the hunter-poet in 'Torn Mountain', for example, or the delightful, motherly artifice evoked in 'Lay of the Fig Tree'.

Bound up with this is Char's apprehension of time, particularly future time. Fittingly for a poet who came of age amid the political chaos of the 1930s, Char had an almost preternatural obsession with what one might call forward-thinking, or the opening-up of time. Like a dying fire, the truth of the world has to be raked out, freed of the ashes and clinker of past time;

or, to use two other images he draws on here, is what is revealed to man in the act of making, a compound of past, present and future which has to be kneaded and leavened like dough ('The Mirage of the Clock Hands') or wrought like iron in the blacksmith's forge ('Frequency'). This is what he was pointing up when he once remarked to Heidegger, 'a poem has no memory; my job is to press ahead'.

There are numerous images for this in his work, together with a whole battery of words starting with *pre-* or *fore-*. One of the loveliest occurs at the end of 'Why the Day Flies', where the poet is likened to a kind of baker's boy, hurrying on ahead to see how the bread has turned out. Elsewhere he reappears, shaman-like, as the 'unnameable beast' at Lascaux, the tragic imagination gravid with the future. And in one of Char's most arresting prose poems, 'The Deadly Sparring-Partner', the birth of a poem is described in terms of a boxing-match between two lovers, in which the poet, like the hunter at Lascaux, has to die to the world in order to free up the future and be born again, in and through the poem.

The other big theme is the clash between the rational consciousness and the twilight zones of the human psyche so beautifully embodied in the French word *ténèbres*. For Char, who once wrote a letter to the editor of *Les Cahiers du Sud*, thanking him for an article on his work, but protesting against the overly virtuous image it conveyed of the poet, man is essentially a desiring creature and, as such, a hunter whose motives can never be either pure or entirely rational. If darkness and daylight are judged to be at odds with each other, then Char, like the screech owl in 'At the Prow of the Roof', will side with the generative, and as yet inviolate, world of night. One of the poems included here is a particularly good illustration of this. 'On the One Axis' starts out from a memory of the Resistance and a paradox worthy of Donne (that the penumbra around a candle is a truer source of illumination than the candle itself), moves on to a description of George de la Tour's work as a metaphor for the sleights of hand of the rational mind, then homes in on the extraordinary image of Descartes' 'exemplary' fountaineer (Descartes and La Tour, let us remember, were almost exact contemporaries), the rational soul ensconced in the brain of a mechanized human body and manipulating the flows of consciousness; a coda then ties this in with an actual political event, the installation of nuclear missiles in Char's native Provence.

I should say a word or two about the making of these translations. Though designed to stand alone as poems that might conceivably have been written in English, they are not what are commonly referred to as 'imitations'. Not because I have any particular quarrel with a genre widely practised by poets today and without which we would have neither Lowell's versions of Baudelaire nor Christian Wiman's marvellous Mandelstam variations. Char, however, is just too singular a poet to be made over in that way, and if he can be translated at all, it has to be on his own terms, I think. I have tried at all times, that is, to stay as close as possible to the French, and when I have departed from the letter of the original, it has been with an ear not only to cadence but, often as not, to the roots of the word as well. The reverse is also true: Char will quite often use a word both in its modern and its root sense, which pretty much forces the hand of the translator; etymologically, the word 'happiness' is bound up with chance, 'enthusiasm' with divine inspiration, and so forth, and to use any other word would sacrifice too much of the meaning. I have also expanded words when necessary. Active, for example, in Char's use of the abstract noun '*étendue*' ('expanse') in 'The Mirage of the Clock Hands' is the more concrete sense of 'taut' or 'stretched flat' ('*tendue*'), which links the image of a bound-less desert waste to the image of Rembrandt's flayed carcass. The latter sense is also present in the roots of the word 'expanse', of course, but in English you don't *hear* it; hence my (tautological, and deliberately so) 'wide-spread expanse'. Similarly, in 'The Last March', the line I have translated as 'Barrows of rubble, banners in rags' unzips two images which, in the French, are compressed into a single metaphor ('*Que de bannières en débris*'). And very occasionally, I have used a slightly different image, one that is cognate with the original, so to speak, but a distant cousin rather than a sibling—'gallery' for 'frieze' in 'The Unnameable Beast', for example, or 'horn-toothed' for the more exotic '*dent déclive*' (literally, 'sloping' or 'inclined') in 'Young Viper'. There are scholars who will quibble about this, no doubt, but for a translator these are among the most rewarding moments of all: when you bring something to a poem which, in a sense, was already there.

Mark Hutchinson
Paris, July 2015

APEMANTUS: Where liest o'nights, Timon?

TIMON: Under that's above me.

SHAKESPEARE, *Timon of Athens*

I know the roads march swiftly on
Unlike the schoolboy traipsing home
His satchel harnessed to his back
As he rambles through the cloying fumes
Of autumn in its breathless fall
Never tender to your subjects
Was it you I now saw smiling
I tremble for you little daughter

Were you not wary after all
Of this wandering stranger
When raising his cap to you
He asked you the way
You didn't seem surprised
You came together like
A poppy and a stalk of corn
I tremble for you little daughter

The flower he holds between his teeth
He could easily dispense with it
If willing to reveal his name
The carcass washed back out to sea
Thereafter some foul confession
That would haunt you in your sleep

Amid the brambles of his blood
I tremble for you little daughter

When the young man went on his way
Your face walled over in the gloaming
When the young man went on his way
Back hunched head down hands empty
Under the willows your face was grave
You had never been that way before
Will he give you back your beauty
I tremble for you little daughter

That flower hanging from his mouth
Do you know what it was hiding
Father a pure evil bordered with flies
I laid my pity on it like a veil
Yet in his eyes was held in troth
The promise I had made myself
I'm foolish yes I'm newly fledged
It's you my father who are changing

I strangled
My brother
Because he hated sleeping
With the window open.

My sister
He said before he died
I've spent entire nights
Watching you sleeping
Brooding on your reflection in the window

The Mill on the Calavon. For two whole years, cicadas sang in the farmhouse, the chateau ran with swifts. Here, everything echoed to the mountain stream, sometimes laughing, sometimes with a young man's fists. Today, his strength failing, the ageing *réfractaire* has only his stones to conjure with, for the most part killed off by frost and loneliness and heat. The omens, too, grow drowsy in the silent flowers.

Roger Bernard: the monsters' horizon lay too close to his lands.

Don't go looking for him in the mountains. But if, a few miles on from there, in the Oppedette Gorge, you should meet the lightning with a schoolboy's face, go to him with a smile, for he must be hungry now, O hungry for friendship.

The lamp came on. Immediately, it was clasped round by a prison yard. Eel fishers would come there to scour the scant grass with their hooks in the hope of extracting the where-withal to bait their lines. The dregs of the entire underworld found succour in this place. And night after night the same little game would be acted out, with myself as nameless witness and victim. I opted for obscurity and reclusion.

Ordinance star. I part the gates to the garden of the dead. Servile flowers are gathered in prayer. Wives of man. Ears of the Creator.

MAGDALENE AT THE NIGHT LIGHT

by Georges de La Tour

I would that the grass were white today: treading it underfoot, I would not have to see you suffer, would not have to see death's hard, unrendered form beneath your young girl's fingers. On a day of your choosing, others, albeit less avid than myself, will remove your linen blouse and inhabit your alcove. On leaving, however, they will forget to douse the night light, and a drop of oil will spill from the flame's dagger onto the impossible solution.

All day long, hand in hand with the blacksmith, the iron bends its torso to the flaming mire of the forge; until finally their twin sinews have freed the metal's slender night from the narrow earth that confined it.

His work done, the blacksmith slowly sets off home. One last time, he plunges his arms into the darkened womb of the river. Will he at last be able to grasp the frozen pouch and staff of algae?

Labour! summoned the blade-lock.
Bleed! the knife echoed back.
My memory was torn from me,
My chaos laid upon the rack.

Those who had loved me once,
Then hated, then forgotten me,
Were leaning at my shoulder once again.
Some were weeping, some were pleased.

Cold sister, harsh December grass,
Walking, I have watched you grow,
A deeper green than memory,
A higher force than any foe.

Oh! the ever more barren solitude
Of the tears which well up on the peaks.

When havoc breaks loose
And a powerless old eagle
Feels confident once more,
Happiness in turn takes wing,
Catching them up from
The brink of the abyss.

Rival hunter, you haven't learnt a thing,
You who press on beyond me in death
To which I give the lie.

Le Rebanqué, Lagnes, 29 August 1949

Time and again, they urged us to accept
A future that in their eyes augured well:
Our blackout to be modelled on their own example,
Our anguish one we knew too well.
We scorned their offers of equality,
To words so sedulous responded No.
We followed the road our hearts had lined with stone
Till we came to the plains of the air and the one silence.
We gave the blood of our uncompromising love,
Our happiness we brought to bear with every pebble.

Today they say the prospect of hail alarms them
More than the dead now falling here like snow.

THE INVENTORS

They came, the foresters from the other side, the unknown
to us, the hostile to our ways.
They came, and they were many.
Their host appeared at the line dividing the cedar woods
From a field long harvested that even now rose fresh and green.
The long march had warmed them.
Their caps broke over their eyes and their tired feet foundered
somewhere distant.

They caught sight of us and halted.
Clearly, they had not thought to find us there,
On a land where the soil was easy and the furrow close,
Quite heedless of an audience.
We raised our heads and beckoned them to come on.

The most fluent among them came over, then a second,
likewise rootless and slow.
We have come, they said, to warn you of the imminent arrival
of the storm, your implacable foe.
What knowledge we have of such things, we have, as you do,
Only on hearsay and from what our ancestors have confided.
Yet why is it we feel so inexplicably happy in your presence,
and so suddenly like children?

We thanked them and sent them once more on their way.
Yet, prior to this, they had drunk, and their hands
    trembled and their eyes laughed at the edges.
Men at home among trees and with axes, able to stand
    their ground before some terrible fear, yet unfit for the
    channelling of water, or the alignment of a building, or its
    coating with pleasant colours,
Of the winter garden they would know nothing, nor of
    the economy of joy.

Undoubtedly we could have convinced and conquered them,
For the anguish before a storm is deeply moving.
And, yes, the storm was shortly to appear.
But was that really something to be talked about and to
    disturb the future for?
At the point we have reached, there are no urgent fears.

Sivergues, 30 September 1949

She has set the table and brought to perfection in her mind what her lover, seated opposite, will later speak to in a whisper, as he gazes into her face: a dish so fine it might be the reed of an oboe.

For the moment, her naked ankles are toying beneath the table with her loved one's warmth, while voices she does not hear pay compliments to her. The weave of the lamp's loom ravels and unravels her: voluptuous, elsewhere.

Its sheets fragrant, its frame shaking, far off, she knows, an exiled bed lies waiting, like a mountain lake that will never be abandoned.

There was a glutton once who gobbled up so much food, wolfed down so many birthrights and sunk his fellow men so deep in poverty that he lost his appetite, lost it forever, and now found his table bare, his bed empty, his wife with child and the soil barren in the field of his heart.

Lacking a grave and eager to join the living, with nothing to give and still less to receive, spurned by the world of objects and lied to by animals, he stole famine and from it concocted a dish that was his mirror and his downfall.

THE DEADLY SPARRING-PARTNER

for Maurice Blanchot

He challenged her, going straight for the heart like a boxer—trim, winged, powerful, nicely centred in the offensive and defensive geometry of his legs. In a glance, he weighed up the strengths of his opponent who, hemmed in between her own pleasing virginity and his experience of the ring, was content to break off fighting. On the white surface where the match was being held, they forgot the pitiless spectators. The forenames of the flowers of the first day of summer fluttered in the June air. Then, at last, his opponent winced slightly and a streak of pink appeared on her cheek. The riposte was brusque and to the point. His legs suddenly like wet linen, the man staggered backwards, afloat. The fists opposing him, however, declined to conclude the match and left it at that. For the moment, the battered heads of the two fighters bobbed together. At which point, the first must deliberately have whispered into the second one's ear something so utterly offensive or appropriate or enigmatic that the latter unleashed a bolt of lightning—immediate, entire, precise—which knocked the incomprehensible fighter out cold.

Some beings have a meaning we lack. Who are they? Their secret is bound up with the secret of life itself. They draw near. Life kills them. But the future they have roused in this way with a murmur, sensing their presence, creates them. O labyrinth of utmost love!

I was nothing more that day than two legs walking.
My eyes vacant, a zero at the centre of my face,
I took to following the stream that ran through the valley.
Low-lying, that dull recluse was not one to intrude
On the wilderness now growing up all round me.

From the cornerstone of a ruin formed once by fire,
Two wild rose shrubs filled with great tenderness and
     determination emerged,
Plunging abruptly down into the grey water.
You could somehow sense the bustle of the departed, the hour
     approaching when they'd once more walk abroad.

The harsh vermillions of a rose, as it struck the water,
In a rapture of questions restored the sky to its original aspect,
Rousing the earth from slumber with its loving tongue
And urging me on into the future, like a famished, feverish tool.

At the next turning, the Epte woods began.
There'd be no need to cross them, though, my beloved
     seed-sowers of recovery!
Half-turning, I breathed a damp must from the meadows
     where a beast was merging;
I heard the slither of the fearful grass snake;

I did then—do not treat me harshly—what all, I knew,
were hoping would be done.

He glides over the moss on a stone, like daylight blinking through a shutter. All he needs is a dewdrop for his head and two twigs to clothe him. Poor soul desperate for a boxwood hedge and one small patch of earth, he's the horn-toothed creature who's doomed to undermine them. Vying with him, his one adversary, is daybreak, who, having fingered the quilt and smiled on the sleeper's hand, lets drop his pitchfork and scurries off to the bedroom ceiling. The sun is the next to arrive, perfecting the work with eager lips.

Cold-blooded, the viper will remain so till rife with death, for the want of a parish makes him a murderer in all men's eyes.

In the course of his lifetime, a poet will lean against a tree, some ocean or slope, a cloud of a certain colour—but only for a moment, and only if circumstances permit. He's not welded fast to someone else's aberrations. His love, his grasp of things, his joy, can all be found in places he has not visited and never will, among strangers he'll never meet. When voices are raised in his presence, honours urged on him that would tie him down, should someone in speaking of him invoke the stars, he replies that his is that *neighbouring* stretch of country where the heavens have just gone down.

The poet quickens, then hurries on ahead to meet the outcome.

At dusk, though dimpled like an apprentice, he's a courteous passer-by who cuts short the farewells to make sure he's present when the bread comes out of the oven.

QU'IL VIVE!

This land is only a wish of the spirit, a counter-sepulchre

In my land, the tender proofs of spring and poorly dressed birds take precedence over distant goals.

Truth waits for dawn beside a candle. The window glass is grimy. To the watchful, it's of no importance.

In my land, you don't question a man who is moved.

No evil shadow falls on the capsized boat.

A grudging good-day is unheard-of in my land.

You borrow only what you can give back with increase.

In my land, the trees have many leaves. Their branches are free not to bear fruit.

Nobody believes in the good faith of the victor.

In my land, we give thanks.

From the muzzle of this gun it snows. Our heads were an inferno. At the same moment, spring is at our fingertips: the open stride at liberty once more, the earth in love, the grasses exuberant.

The spirit, too, like all things, trembled.

The eagle is infutured.

Any act that engages the soul, even when the latter is unaware of it, will have repentance or sorrow as its epilogue. You have to consent to that.

How did writing come to me then? Like bird's down on my window pane, in winter. Immediately, a battle of firebrands sprang up in the hearth which is still not over, even now.

Silken towns gazed on daily, nested in other towns, their streets marked out by ourselves alone and shielded by bursts of lightning responsive to our overtures.

Our whole being should be one big joyous feast when something we have not foreseen and can shed no light on, which will later speak to our heart, comes about of its own accord.

Let us continue taking soundings, speaking in level tones, with words in close formation: we will eventually silence all these dogs, have them melt back into the meadows, where they will keep a bleary eye on us as their backs are rubbed out by the wind.

Lightning lasts me.

Only my fellow human being, friend or lover, can rouse me from my torpor, set poetry in motion and pit me against the confines of the ancient wilderness that I might overcome them. Nothing else. No heaven, no chosen land, none of the things that stir us.

Only with them does my beacon waltz.

You cannot embark on a poem without a morsel of error regarding yourself and the world, without a mote of innocence in the first few words.

In a poem, nearly every word should be used in its original sense. Some break away and take on multiple meanings. Others suffer from amnesia. The constellation of Solitarius is tightly strung.

Poetry will cheat me of my death.

Why *pulverized poem*? Because at the end of its voyage up-country, after the prenatal darkness and the harshness of earthly existence, a poem's finitude is light, the bringing of being to life.

A poet doesn't hold on to what he discovers; having set it down in writing, he soon grows out of it. Therein lies his novelty, his boundlessness and his peril.

My profession? Jutting-edge . . .

We are born with men, we die unconsoled among the gods.

The earth that accepts the seed is sad. The seed which has so much to lose is happy.

There's a malediction unlike any other. It flickers in a kind of idleness, has a comely nature and puts on a reassuring face. But what gusto once the pretence is over, how promptly it hastens to its goal! Since the shadow where it builds is malicious, the very zone of secrecy, it will probably defy naming, will always slip away in time. The parables it outlines on the veil of the sky of a few clairvoyant souls are rather terrifying.

Books which don't move. But books which slip easily into our days, utter a lament, open the dance.

How can I put it, the freedom and surprise I feel after all these detours: there *is* no bedrock; there *is* no ceiling.

From time to time the silhouette of a young horse or a distant child comes up as a pathfinder to my front and jumps the barrier of my concern. Then under the trees the fountain speaks once more.

We wish to remain unknown to the curiosity of our loved ones. We love them.

Light has an age. Night does not. But in what instant did that fully formed fountainhead arise?

Not to have several deaths pending, as though blanketed in snow. To have just one, of good sand. And no resurrection.

Let us pause for a moment among those who can cut themselves off from their resources, though for them there can be little or no falling back. The long wait leaves them reeling from insomnia. Beauty crowns them with a hat of flowers.

Birds who entrust your slenderness and your hazardous sleep to a bundle of reeds, how like you we are when the cold sets in!

I admire the hands that plenish, and, for matching and joining, the finger that discards the thimble.

It occurs to me at times that the current of our existence is all but impossible to trace, for not only are we subject to its whimsical ways, but the easy movement of the arms and legs which would get us to where we would gladly go, to the coveted shore and new loves whose differences would enrich us, remains incomplete and quickly dwindles into an image, like a ball of scent hanging over our thoughts.

As desire, desire that knows, any advantage we derive from the twilight zones of the human psyche depends on a few truly sovereign powers bound up with invisible flames, and invisible chains, which, in revealing themselves, little by little, make us shine.

Beauty makes its sublime bed all alone, builds its fame strangely among men: nearby, but off to one side.

Let us sow reeds and grow wine on the hillsides, cheek by jowl with the wounds of our spirit. Cruel fingers, careful hands, this jovial spot augurs well.

He who invents, unlike he who discovers, adds nothing to the world, brings nothing to his fellow men but masks and middlings, iron gruel.

Life in its entirety at last when I pluck your gentle love-truth from your deeps!

Stay close to the cloud. Keep close watch on the implement. All seed is hateful.

The beneficence of men some strident mornings. Into the swarming, delirious air I rise, I shut myself in, an insect undevoured, pursuing and pursued.

Faced with the harsh forms of these waters, where all the flowers of the green mountain drift by in loose bouquets, the Hours marry themselves to gods.

Chill sun, I its climbing vine.

There was so much frost that winter
That the milky branches mauled the saw
Or snapped in two. Come spring,
The gracious ones would not turn green.

Of the master of the fallen wood
The fig tree asked a flourishing new faith.
And lo, like a fiery prophet come to tell
Of new life dawning, an oriol appeared;
Yet, alighting on the ill-starred tree,
Succumbed, not to hunger but to love.

LASCAUX

I. DEAD BIRD-MAN, DYING BISON

The long body, once urgent and enthused,
Perpendicular at present to the wounded Brute.

A man without entrails, dead.
Beside him, healed by the hunter's death,
She who was all to him once, the bison, dying.

High over the depths he dances,
The birth-hungry, the deathless bird.
Froward the fruit culled from the shaman's branch,
Hard-won his haven.

II. BLACK STAGS

The sky still listened when the waters spoke.
Up from the dark rocks, into the air's caress,
The stags come, fording the millenia.

The guardian eye of genius, the hunter's goad:
I stand on the wide shore, marvelling at their passion.
And if, in the moment of hope, I had their eyes?

III. THE UNNAMEABLE BEAST

The unnameable Beast rounds off the graceful herd,
    like a comic cyclops.
Eight jibes adorn her and divide her folly.
The Beast belches devoutly in the country air.
Her heavy, hanging flanks are aching and must
    empty their charge.
From her hooves to the horns that helplessly defend her,
    a rank scent surrounds her.

Comes to me thus, in the great gallery at Lascaux,
Mother inconceivably disguised,
Wisdom, her eyes filled with tears.

IV. YOUNG HORSE WITH HAZY MANE

Here is the gorgeous pony, Spring,
Riddling the sky with her mane,
Splashing the reeds with foam.
Every name that Love puts on
Is there in her long, full neck:
From the White Lady of Africa
To Magdalene at the Mirror:
The idol who strikes back,
The pensiveness of grace.

ON THE ONE AXIS

I. THE JUST VISION OF GEORGES DE LA TOUR

26 January, 1966

The only way to avoid beating an interminable retreat was to enter the circle of the candle and to abide by it, fighting off the temptation to replace darkness with daylight, and its unwavering penumbra with a more variable term.

He opens his eyes. It's daylight, they say. Georges de La Tour knows that the doomed man's barrow is everywhere making its way, an artful consignment on board. The vehicle has overturned. The painter draws up the inventory. Nothing that belongs everlastingly to night and to the glowing tallow that extols its line is to be found mixed in among the goods. One hand behind his back, the trickster, at once brazen and sly, pulls an ace of diamonds from his belt; the beggar minstrels are brawling among themselves, the stake is worth scarcely more than the knife that's about to strike; the fortune being told is not the first offence of a wayward young gypsy; syphilitic, blind, his neck flaking with scrofula, the vielle-player intones an inaudible purgatory. Daylight, the exemplary fountaineer of all our ills. Georges de La Tour was not mistaken.

II. THE RUIN OF ALBION

24 February, 1966

Let those who bore into Albion's noble crust take note of this: we are fighting for a *site* where snow is not only the she-wolf in winter but also the alder tree in spring. The sun rises there on our uncompromising blood and no man is ever prisoner among his kind. In our eyes, this *site* is of more value than the bread we share, for, unlike bread, nothing can replace it.

With my teeth
I took life
On the knife of my youth.
With my lips today,
With my lips alone . . .

Curt parvenu,
The wayside flower,
Orion's Barb,
Puts forth once more.

They mistake for clarity the hollow laughter of the inferno. They weigh in their hands the remains of death and cry: 'It's not for us.' No treasured provisions embellish the jaws of their uncoiled snakes. Their wives cheat on them, their children rob them, their friends mock them. They notice none of this, in their hatred of the dark. The lights thrown by the diamond of creation happen to be oblique? Quick, then: a decoy to cover it over. They thrust into their oven and leaven the limp dough of their bread with the merest smidgen of despair. They have set up shop and thrive in the bower of a sea where they have commandeered the glaciers. You have been warned.

How, poor schoolboy, are you to win round the future and rake out this fire you have questioned and poked at often enough, once fallen upon your sheepish gaze?

The present is just a game, a bowmen's massacre.

As faithful to his love then as the sky is to the rock. Faithful, sulfured, but ceaselessly roaming, concealing his path through the wide-spread expanse disclosed by fire, gripped round by wind; the expanse, the butcher's hoard, bleeding on a hook.

The pillow's scarlet, the pillow's black,
Side-on in sleep, one breast bare,
And nothing between, from star to square,
But barrows of rubble, banners in rags!

Cut through and have done with you,
While the must is in the vat, fermenting,
And trust in the sunburst lips to come.

Nave now to the underlying air
That hardens the waters of the white marshes,
Suffering, with sufferance, at last put by,
And at one with the chill of language,
I will summon the warm rim to rise.

Two riverbanks are needed for truth: one for our outward journey, the other for truth's return. Paths that soak up their mist. That preserve our merry laughter intact. That, even when broken, are a haven for our juniors, swimming in icy waters.

What expert barbarity will be only too glad of us tomorrow? Know that what existed in the past now lies ahead, like an orchid in a winter garden, bleeding from a caesarean.

Between the telescope and the microscope, that is our position now, in a raging sea, at the heart of the great divide, bracing ourselves, pushing back—pitiless, unwanted guests.

The failure of philosophy and tragic art: a failure of benefit to no one but applied science, that gem-setter turned scheming old slag, hunched over her stewing-pan, who for all her deathly masks and fancy dress, now acts as the go-between in our hybrid, commonplace lives.

There are those who drank of Marat's bath-water, and those, like ourselves, who shuddered on the horizon of Lenin and Saint-Just. Stalin, however, is perpetually in the offing. Hitler's jaw-bone is piously preserved. Can anything deflect our bodies from the laser's pellagric beam? Oh! the unseemliness of a sound mind, faced with a sea full of poison ivy!

'To gnaw' is one of the few verbs that can be conjugated in pitch darkness. The excellence of the tooth's hungry work! And how right the object being flayed is to rejoice in its fate. It purrs with pleasure. Gnawing is a ritualization of death.

Subordination or terror, then the two together, is the totalitarianism on which everything is now converging: the wilderness as wedding ring, the sinister manoeuverings, the penal interludes . . . Blind men, don't go pissing on the glow-worm; he alone still hastens on his way.

An authoritarian science breaks ranks with its self-effacing sisters and scoffs at the miracle of life, transforming it into a currency based on fear. It's the same old story, the object debased by the idea. The beast has become a creature of legend, a spume of foam . . .

Man identical to man, man ground infinitesimally small, is the spectre that materialism, following on from idealism, calls on to endure. The slave identical to the slave, that is, with less and less winnowing.

★

In taking leave of the world, we return to what was out there before the earth and stars were formed; to space, that is. We *are* that space, in all its prodigality. We return to aerial day and its black rejoicing.

This being stretched almost to breaking point between the spirit that is willing and the step that falters. Grind down the obstacle. After the endless fall, we lie there flattened on the ground. We go on living, we learn.

The simpleton has laid out on the parquet where he walks thousands of tin tacks whose jagged heads bruise and bloody his feet. It's the price he has decided to pay for his standing station.

The eagerness with which we lovingly refute Nietzsche for no other reason than that we come after him and that his ravaged site is once again available, exactly as he described it.

When I was young, the world was a blank white wilderness where glaciers rose up in rebellion. Today, it's a bruised and swollen wilderness where even the most gifted soul is master of nothing but his own self-importance.

★

What pests they are, these sons of ours who are too much in the news! Cutting the supply lines to our inheritance is *not* the answer.

To survive, we need our precise complement of emotions. One emotion too many—to lighten another's load, as a token of the hopes they have placed in us, for example—means defeat.

These rain-drenched shepherds are nothing if not efficient!

Under their watchful eye, the ewes huddle together in the gale, like fertile, weary stars, level with the earth.

A newborn lamb is no reason to break off the march.

O the new spirit infused by whosoever sees a single spark entering the furrow of day! We must learn to strike flints at dawn once more, to stem the flow of words.

Words alone, words that are loving, concrete, vengeful, flint-like once again, their echoes nailed to the shutters of houses.

The moment you understand your enemy, and satisfy yourself, without begrudging him the fact, that your enemy hears what you are saying, you are done for.

Grapes have, for their native soil,
The hands of the harvest girl.
But she, who does she have,
With the narrow path and the vineyard, harsh, behind her?

The rosary each cluster makes;
At dusk, the topmost fruit that, setting, sheds
One final spark.

Night of 17th September, 1976. The vault lies open. (My own observations are of no interest on this particular occasion.) The awesome heavenly machinery is in place. Tonight, like an Amazon headhunter lost at a motorway intersection, the moon will have only an unobtrusive role to play. For all my long-standing nausea, my head, which it is becoming increasingly difficult to raise, will see all the demented ladies up there offering their ideal targets to the nimble earthly fornicators. Let us lie down in the damp grass and see for ourselves. Where, then, is the Master Mechanic to be found in all this? This is not at all how things happen on earth. The Great Helmsman, the Father of the Nation, the Statesman of Genius, the Insatiable Democrat, come about of their own accord, with only a little help from a conniving universal suffrage which throws filthy shadows. In the immense community of the heavenly clock face, the Master Mechanic, it would seem, has greased the motors and slipped away, chuckling, to amuse himself elsewhere. Eager suddenly to be up and doing, I hurried off to read *Mes Inscriptions* by that much-loved individual Louis Scutenaire. In no way demented, in no way indulgent towards the joint-purchasers of the allotments of the air, these I read with my head down, one stem at a time—the reading of a rye-field forever green, adjacent to that of the Irishman Swift. A world in which the hedgehog's circulating soul can sprawl at leisure, then scurry off amid the delights of getting gone for good.

Rest at last, then? The life-raft? We fall. I write to you in the midst of my descent. That is my experience of being-in-the-world. Mankind is coming apart just as surely as it was once composed. The wheel of destiny is running backwards and its teeth are tearing us apart. Our rate of acceleration is such that we shall soon catch fire. Love, that sublime brake, is broken, of no use any more.

None of this is written on the sky they have set aside for us, nor in the book we yearn for, as it hurries forward to the rhythm of our heartbeat, then shatters, while our heart continues beating.

—So what is your loved one up to, now that, the house completed, you're laying out a flower bed, enlarging an alley of dwarf gravel and embroidering the night sky as a skullcap for his head?

—Surveying the land, he has other affairs to comfort him: he digs ditches, inveigles walls, dreams of a grey horse stamping its hooves under the apple boughs.

Through sky-blue spectacles, aspiring Spring looks down on winter with the dark sienna eyes. Rise early and you will find them together. A word, then, while the gift is fresh. The first of the day's folds held three villages in the mist. Before long, the Ventoux had brushed the sun back from the gigantic cradle where three of his children lay sleeping, swaddled in tiles; a sun that would name the cradle sovereign, rising in the East, then riverine, bathing it in light once more before departing.

From the belfry of the run-down church, time's banished footman hammered out the hour.

—I hear him moan with pleasure
If he scoops up in his iron clasp,
Leading lightly as she dances,
The dear child who was halt before;

This fresh young water night confers,
Would you, Well, with your weight of years,
Perhaps know who is truly hers?

—He who had kept the middle way
Stumbled on the darkened path
And was parted from his darling.

I hear rain even when it's not the rain,
Just nightfall;
I rejoice in dawn even when it's not the dawn,
But my own white pulp stirring among the mud.
A child's mouth ruffles me with its teeth.
Love of the silent waters!

The hawthorn has the nightingale.
I have the spells that bind.

If they credit me with their evil realities and unimaginable dreams, it's the better to exclude me, is it not? The moment some paltry scrap of fennel frees them to point a rifle at me, they dignify me as 'mad'. Observe the questioning shadows that fall across the chapped lips of their lands . . . Threaded with the sounds of our destruction, they're a more fitting vehicle for the vengeance of my kind than this green wind where a seed flits by.

Since I am the one who watches over the golden realms that fall open at his feet, Orion, striding along by the marshes, would never think me churlish, let alone take me captive in my exhausted sleep.

I have sealed their ginger-haired devil in a bottle and shall offer it to the waves. The ground-swell Claude Lorrain heard encroaching on the piers of his palaces will carry it out to sea.

It was in December, when the nights dress early. An unruly rain had got itself entangled in an icy wind and was taking stabs at it. In a copse nearby, hunters were hiding, one knee poised on the twigs beneath them. Their migratory game in this dismal weather was a flight of panicking thrushes; the marksmen's eyes, on these rich lands of theirs where the plots were too neatly aligned, imagined the birds at sunset, in a hurry to die.

Riverbeds are zealous but very cold.

At the prow of the roof, the screech owl,
With her accustomed eye,
Sees daybreak darkening the prize
That night left unensnared.

After the quartered echo,
The mulberry trees torn up;
The bird whose heart alone perspires
Foreshadows a cruel half-light,
The sky that lit up Corinth in flames.

Our sufferings are one
And the wind is much too light,
The wind with its Medusa's head,
That in Martigues once, pining for childhood,
I mistook for the cry of a bird
Alerting the cindery vault.

Tigron, my friend, soon you'll be a full-grown cherry tree, and nothing will remain of those knowing looks you would give me, nor of the trembling handle of your muzzle, nor of those barks of warning, never tiresome, you would send out left and right. Which direction had we decided on? I was in and out all through your youth, with the risk that you, too, after a long life at my side, would one day be forgotten, anonymous head. Yet now, at the end of it all, a field comes into view that would weep were I to cross it! Neither heedful nor indifferent. While I, on your heart which was beating much too fast, would read: inevitable parting of the ways.

Ah! convention falls from the man who, on the mirror stolen from his home, sees only the two words 'enter' and 'die', yet is anything but gloomy. Is convinced, at least, that he will never see it back. Affection, my friend!

From the all-too-sudden and short-lived trill of the warbler, a word like a cry from the throat shot forth, an elusive trapeze: the word 'hold-up'.

Then silence, and, as though it had vanished, the tree in which it had been singing was once more barren.

It was so hot that summer that even the dead leaves came to drink from the earthenware dishes put down for the dogs.

TO M. H.

11 September, 1966

Back and forth goes Autumn, swifter than the gardener's rake.
Autumn does not overwhelm the heart, which needs the
branch and the branch's shadow.

—Who'd think of building houses on the Pont du Gard?

—Why, the Romans would, if any still survive.

—You have no real feeling for the olive branch.

—I live. The snow hears nothing underneath the hut.

NOTES

Introduction. 'arresting [. . .] inscriptions': Char inscribed an offprint of Celan's translation of *Feuillets d'Hypnos*, '*à Paul Celan, à qui je pensais*' ('for Paul Celan, of whom I was thinking'). Celan's biographer John Felstiner calls this 'the perfect tribute, as though a Resistance testament was looking ahead to its (German-speaking) translator' (in *Paul Celan: Poet, Survivor, Jew*, New Haven and London: Yale University Press, 1995).

'little-known version': Heaney's version of '*L'Adolescent soufffleté*' was privately printed, under the title *The Playground*, in 2005 for the friends of Menard Press, to mark the seventieth birthday of Daniel Weissbort.

'Heracletian notion of strife': the influence of Heraclitus on Char's thinking dates from the early 1930s. He may also have been influenced by the 'infernal wisdom' of Blake's *The Marriage of Heaven and Hell*, a passage from which (in André Gide's translation, slightly modified) he used as an epigraph to his first book, *Les Cloches sur le Cœur* (1928). The emotional roots of that belief can probably be traced back to two events in his childhood: the death of his father in 1918, and the beatings he received from his much older brother for some years afterwards. Char was seven when his father first showed signs of the illness that was to kill him four years later, and his death seems to have been bound up for ever after in Char's mind with the horrors of the First World War. (Char's home town lost 220 lives in the conflict, and Char's father, who was mayor at the time, took it upon himself to inform each family personally of their loss.) As for the beatings he received from his brother, Char's response was to go down to the garden at dawn and box the trunks of trees until he was strong enough to stand up to him. This coalescence of public and private, of violence without and conflict within, partly accounts, in my view, for the intensity of Char's identi-fication with the Resistance. It should also be noted that his brother was a militant Pétainist.

'a small but striking book of translations': *La Planche de vivre* (Paris: Gallimard, 1981).

'who once wrote a letter': 'To hell with truth, for goodness sake! If I occasionally go too far in embracing a certain conduct in life, it's because I'm obsessed with the death of man, the ease with which he falls to pieces. Had I been living in 1850, I wouldn't have had the same anxieties! And I wouldn't have given a damn about society' (letter to Jean Ballard, in *René Char Jean Ballard, Correspondence*, Rougerie Éditeur, 1993).

'Where liest o'nights, Timon?': the lines in question were used by Char as the epigraph to *Les Matinaux* (1950).

The Schoolgirl's Companion. Char's use of the ballad form, for the first and only time in his work, was probably inspired by Lorca, whom he was reading at the time. There are also echoes of Goethe's famous poem, 'Der Erlkrönig' (The

Alder King), which was translated into French by Gérard de Nerval. The poem, written shortly after the bombing of Guernica in April 1937, first appeared in *Placard pour un chemin des écoliers*, a chapbook published by Guy Lévis Mano in December 1937 and dedicated 'to the children of Spain'. (Picasso's *Guernica* was first shown in public in the Spanish Pavilion at the Paris World Fair in July of the same year, an event Char is likely to have attended.) The expression '*prendre le chemin des écoliers*' means to take the long way round.

Anguish, Gunfire, Silence. 'Roger Bernard': a young poet and printer who was a member of Char's Resistance group. His execution by the SS is evoked in fragment 138 of Char's war journal, *Feuillets d'Hypnos*.

réfractaire: the term used in Nazi-occupied France for young Frenchmen who refused to register for the Service du Travail Obligatoire (STO), a forced labour scheme that required all Frenchmen between the ages of twenty-one and thirty to carry out civilian work in Germany. In exchange, the Nazis allowed a number of French military prisoners of war to return home. Many *réfractaire*s joined the Resistance.

'Oppedette': The Gorges d'Oppedette are a group of wooded limestone cliffs a few miles to the north of the field in which Bernard was executed.

Magdalene at the Night Light. 'Madeleine à la Veilleuse' (also called in English *Magdalene with the Smoking Flame*, and on view at the Louvre) is one of several paintings by Georges de la Tour (1593–1652) on the theme of the penitent Magdalene. Char is thought to have discovered La Tour's work at an exhibition of realist painting, held in Paris in 1934.

Frequency. As a child, Char was fascinated by the labours of a local blacksmith who would cool his arms in the river in the evening after finishing work.

'pouch and staff': the traditional attributes of the pilgrim, here invested with sexual undertones.

Labyrinth. The verb I have translated as 'Labour!' is 'Pioche!' (from *piocher*; literally, to break up the earth with a pick or mattock). This was the nickname of René Obadia, one of the hardened military advisers in Char's Resistance group (cf. *Hypnos*, fragment 217).

Torn Mountain. '*29 August, 1949*': the date on which the Soviet Union tested its first atomic bomb.

The Lords of Maussane. 'Maussane': a village in the vallée des Baux, near Arles, renamed Maussane-les-Alpilles in 1968.

'prospect of hail': the expression Char uses ('*au-delà de leur vue*') is unusual and a bit cumbersome in French and may come from Montaigne, who uses the same construction ('Qui verrait au-delà, il verrait au-delà de sa vue' / 'He who should see beyond that, should see further than his sight') in a well-known passage in the *Essays* (Book Two, Chapter 17, 'On Presumption').

The poem was written in 1949, and the closing image of the 'neige des morts' may be an allusion to one of the first major international crises of the Cold War, the Berlin Blockade (1948–49), when seventy Allied pilots died, largely as a result of hazardous weather conditions caused by an unusually harsh winter.

The Inventors. cf. *Hypnos*, fragment 127: The French text is printed with the place and date of composition—*Sivergues, 30 septembre 1949.* Cf. *Hypnos*, fragment 127: 'Like a sleepwalker, man advances towards the murderous mine-fields, led on by the song of the inventors . . .' The almost conversational style of this poem, which was written in 1949, is unusual in Char's work and may owe something to Cavafy. The latter's influence is entirely plausible. Fifteen of Marguerite Yourcenar's translations of Cavafy (including '*En Attendant les Barbares*') were published in 1944 in the review *Fontaine*—an important Resistance journal founded in Algiers, which published a long extract from Char's *Feuillets d'Hypnos* the following year. And in 1948, against the background of the Greek Civil War, Cavafy figured prominently in a special issue, 'Permanence de la Grèce', of *Les Cahiers du Sud*—again, a review Char had close ties with.

The Deadly Sparring-Partner. 'Maurice Blanchot' (1907–2003): an influential French writer and literary theoretician whose work Char particularly admired.

The Epte Woods. 'The Epte': a river in Normandy. In the 1950s, Char stayed regularly at the home of Mme Marion, mother of Yvonne Zervos, at Saint-Clair-sur-Epte. A close friend and lover of Char's at the time, Yvonne Zervos was the wife of the art-historian Christian Zervos, publisher of the *Cahiers d'Art* series, and the director of the gallery of the same name in Paris.

Qu'il Vive! The title is awkward in English. Literally: '[Long] may it live!'

The Library is on Fire. The title, *La Bibliothèque est en feu*, was a coded message used to announce a parachute-drop to Char's Resistance group on 1 May 1944. As related in fragment 53 of *Hypnos*, the first container exploded when it hit the ground, setting fire to the surrounding shrubbery and woods. Following this incident, Char asked for gelig-nite to be replaced by plastic explosive, which is triggered by a detonator. Legend also has it that, alarmed by the coincidence of word and event, he asked for the message to be changed.

'pulverized poem': *Le poème pulvérisé* is the title of a chap-book Char published in 1947.

'jutting-edge': there's a play on words in Char's use of the expression, *métier de pointe*—literally, 'cutting-edge profession'; figuratively, an allusion to the deictic character of poetry, in which the function of language is not to spell out or explain but to indicate, point up, show. In old French, 'pointe' is also used of the point of a weapon or the vanguard of an army.

'the Hours marry themselves to gods': the three Greek Ὧραι, (*Hōrai*), more commonly referred to as the Seasons in English, were the daughters of Zeus and Themis, and were identified with budding, growing and fruiting. They are usually represented holding a flower or a plant.

Lay of the Fig Tree. The 'back-story' of this poem concerns a particularly harsh winter in the wake of which, to make up for the fruit not ripening, Char bought a packet of dried figs, soaked them in milk and hung them from the tree in question.

Lascaux. 'Magdalene at the Mirror': a painting by Georges de la Tour (see note to 'Magdalene at the Night Light'), usually called 'The Repentant Magdalene' in English and today in the National Gallery of Art in Washington.

'The White Lady of Africa': a rock painting in the Brandberg massif in Namibia, depicting a warrior-like female figure. Discovered in 1918, it was given the name by Abbé Henri Breuil, the anthropologist who was the first to explore the painted cave complex discovered at Lascaux in 1940. Breuil believed the figure revealed communication between the Mediterranean and southern Africa; today, it is generally considered to be a bushman painting.

'eyes filled with tears': cf. Montaigne's 'On Democritus and Heraclitus' (*Essays*, Book One), where Heraclitus is described as wearing 'a face perpetually sad, and eyes filled with tears'.

The scenes evoked in the four poems, which first appeared in *Les Cahiers d'Art* in 1952, are also discussed at some length in George Bataille's book, *Lascaux: ou la naissance de l'art*, first published in 1955. It is likely that the two men, who were friends and lived not far from each other at the time, discussed their responses to the cave paintings.

On the One Axis. Georges de la Tour: see note to 'Magdalene at the Night Light'. The poem draws on four of La Tour's paintings: *Le Tricheur* ('The Cheat', Musée du Louvre, Paris); *La Diseuse de Bonne Aventure* ('The Fortune-Teller,' Metroplitan Museum of Art, New York); *Le Joueur de Vielle* ('The Hurdy-Gurdy Player', Museo Nacional del Prado, Madrid); and *Rixe des Musiciens* ('The Musicians' Brawl', J. Paul Getty Museum, Los Angeles).

'fountaineer' : cf. Descartes, *Treatise on Man* : 'And finally, when a rational soul is present in this machine [the body] it will have its principal seat in the brain and will reside there like the fountaineer who must be stationed at the tanks to which the fountain's pipes return if he wants to initiate, impede or in some way alter their movements'.

'Albion': in 1966, Char played an active role in protests against the installation of part of France's strategic nuclear arsenal on the Plateau d'Albion, an expanse of sparsely populated table-land at the foot of the Mont Ventoux. Eighteen underground silos and three missile-launch control centres were installed there between 1966 and 71, before being dismantled in the late 1990s.

Dumb Show. 'Orion's barb': according to the late Tina Jolas, *dard d'Orion* was the name given in Provence to a small wayside flower; according to one of Char's translators, Prithwindra Mukherjee, it is a type of cactus flower which Char had growing in his garden.

The Mirage of the Clock Hands. 'sulfured': in traditional wine-making, barrels are disinfected with the fumes from a burning linen wick soaked in sulfur.

'butcher's hoard, bleeding on its hook': an allusion to the Rembrandt painting in the Louvre, 'Carcass of Beef' (or 'Flayed Ox'). Elsewhere, Char calls the painting the 'only sun' that is left to us today.

Loins. The French text is part of a sequence based around the figure of Orion, the giant hunter of Greek mythology, and is printed with the following running outline beneath the title: '*Orion swims across the Eridanos and confronts the Hydra*'. In the Bible, the loins are often associated with spiritual resolve. 'currency based on fear': during the French Revolution, the bells of Notre Dame and other churches were melted down for coin and cannon.

'the laser's pellagric beam'. Pellagra, a deadly vitamin-deficiency disease caused by undernourishment, was widespread in the Soviet gulags. In the Chronology to his collected poems, Char cites, for the year 1969, the French publication of Varlam Shalamov's *Article 58*, an account of the author's incarceration in Soviet labour camps, '*livre atrocement inoubliable*'.

Fontis. A doline crater or sinkhole (a depression formed in karst terrain when the ceiling of a subterranean gallery collapses). According to a note in Char's collected poems, they are often used in Provence to plant grape vines.

How Did I Ever Get This Late. '17th September, 1976': the date on which NASA unveiled the space shuttle *Enterprise*.

Louis Scutenaire (1905–87): a Belgian Surrealist poet.

Bell Glass. 'Ventoux': the Mont Ventoux, a mountain in the Vaucluse region, visible from the poet's home in the Isle-sur-Sorgue. It is associated with Petrarch, who climbed the mountain in 1336 and, much later, wrote a well-known letter describing the ascent, in which he claimed to have been the first person to climb the mountain since antiquity.

The March Hare's Vindication. Claude Lorrain: Claude Gellée (1604/5?–82), called Claude (or, in France, Le Lorrain), a French painter famous for his depictions of idealized landscapes and imaginary seaports framed by classical buildings, often in ruins.

At the Prow of the Roof. 'Corinth in flames': the ancient city-state of Corinth was razed to the ground after a ferocious battle in 146 BC that marked the beginning of Roman hegemony over Greece. The site was resettled as a Roman colony around 44 BC.

The Mighty Jumper. 'Tigron': the poet's dog. *Tigron* is French for 'tigon', the offspring of a tiger and a lioness.

Newsletter. Nouvelles à la main were an early form of journalism, handwritten newsletters commissioned by prominent individuals (government officials, merchants, bankers) to keep themselves informed about political and economic developments. They were widely used for propaganda purposes during the sixteenth-century wars of religion.

To M. H.: the initials and date commemorate the death of the German philosopher Martin Heidegger. Char was first introduced to Heidegger's work by Tristan Tzara's ex-wife, Greta Knutson, a highly educated Swedish artist and writer with whom he had a long and passionate affair in the late 1930s. The two men first met during a visit Heidegger made to Paris in 1955 and later held a series of informal seminars (1966–73) at Le Thor, a small town on the banks of the Sorgue. Char never called into question the 'official' French account of Heidegger's involvement with the Nazi

Party in the 1930s and shortly before his death had a falling-out with Maurice Blanchot over the matter. While Char and Heidegger shared a passionate interest in the pre-Socratic philosophers and a deep mistrust of the technological turn taken by the West, Char did not read German and his engagement with Heidegger's work is unlikely to have been of the same order as Celan's. As he once told an admirer: 'I have nothing to do with Heidegger's philosophy. I'm a poet, not a philosopher in verse. . . . [Heidegger] mainly interested me when he trained his telescope on the [ancient] Greeks.' (Paul Veyne, *René Char en ses poèmes*, Paris: Gallimard, 1990).

Hut. The Pont du Gard: an ancient Roman aqueduct near Nîmes, in the south of France, famed for the engineering prowess underlying its construction.

★

These poems were first published in the following:

In *Les Matinaux* © Editions Gallimard, 1950:
'Qu'il vive!', 'Les Inventeurs', 'Les Seigneurs du Maussane', 'Le Masque
funèbre', 'L'Amoureuse en secret', 'Montagne déchirée', 'Dédale'.

In *La parole en archipel* © Editions Gallimard, 1962:
'Mortel partenaire', 'Pourquoi la journée vole', 'Fontis', 'Le Bois de l'Epte',
'La Bibilothèque est en feu', 'Lascaux (I–IV)', 'Le viperau'.

In *Fureur et mystère* © Editions Gallimard, 1962:
'Fréquence', 'Violences', '[Conduite]', '[La Compagne du vannier]',
'Madeleine à la veilleuse', 'Affres détonation silence'.

In *Le nu perdu* © Editions Gallimard, 1971:
'Lied du Figuier', 'Sur un même axe', 'Jeu Muet', '[Mirage des aiguilles]',
'Dernière marche', 'A M. H.'

In *Aromates chasseurs* © Editions Gallimard, 1975:
'Vindicte due Lièvre', 'Lombes', 'Pontonniers'.

In *Chants de la Balandrane* © Editions Gallimard, 1977:
'Verrine', 'Le seau échoué', 'Le jonc ingénieux'.

In *Fenêtres dormantes et portes sur le toit* © Editions Gallimard, 1979
'Comment ai-je pu prendre un tel retard', 'Légèreté de la terre',
'Les vents galactiques'.

In *Les voisinages de Van Gogh* © Editions Gallimard, 1985:
'Le Bon Sauteur', 'Société'.

In *Placard pour un chemin des écoliers*, GLM 1937, et *Oeuvres complètes*
© Editions Gallimard, 1983:
'[Quatre Ages]'.

In *Eloge d'une soupçonnée* © Editions Gallimard, 1988:
'Nouvelles à la main', 'Cabane'.

Jean Baudrillard, *Carnival and Cannibal,*
Or The Play of Global Antagonism
TRANSLATED BY CHRIS TURNER

Tzvetan Todorov, *Torture and the War on Terror*
TRANSLATED BY GILA WALKER

Pablo Picasso and Gertrude Stein, *Correpondence*
TRANSLATED BY LORNA SCOTT FOX

Ninar Esber, *Conversations with My Father, Adonis*
TRANSLATED BY LORNA SCOTT FOX

Jean-Paul Sartre, *The Aftermath of War*
TRANSLATED BY CHRIS TURNER

Georges Bataille, Michel Leiris, *Correspondence*
TRANSLATED BY LIZ HERON

Guy Debord, *A Sick Planet*
TRANSLATED BY DONALD NICHOLSON-SMITH